# Juices & Smoothies

## COLOFON

**Recipes** Thea Spierings **Editor/Final editing** Maaike van Helmond **Design** Sabine van Loon, Myrthe Bergboer **Styling** Tonnie van Doorn **Photography** Food4Eyes.com, Freek Stoltenborgh **Assistant publisher** Josje Kets **Publisher** Pieter Harts **With thanks to** SOLIS

© Visconti

© This edition: Miller Books
e-mail info@miller-books.com
www.miller-books.com

1st printing 2008
ISBN 978 90 8724 054 7

No part of this book may be reproduced in any form or by an electronic or mechanical means, including information storage or retrieval devices or systems, without prior written permission from the publisher.

Disclaimer: Information in this book is not intended as medical advice but as supplementary information only. Always consult your physician for medical advice and before embarking upon a liquid fast.

"Nothing beats the taste of freshly squeezed vegetable and fruit juices. They are the ideal and delicious way to get your vitamins!"

Thea Spierings is a high-profile chef for the culinary magazine Wining & Dining and has several cookbooks to her name.

Thea worked for many years as a chef in various prestigious restaurants and has been nominated for Female Chef of the Year.

Her passion for cooking is evident in her practical and inspiring recipes.

# FOREWORD

Fresh juice drinks and smoothies are extremely tempting. They look good, smell wonderful, and are also easy and quick to make. And as a bonus, most juice drinks and smoothies are filled to the brim with wholesomeness. There is no end to variations and combinations of ingredients. Juice drinks and smoothies can be whatever you want them to be, which means you can be adventurous and create your own recipes!

What exactly are juice drinks and smoothies, or rather, what is the difference between the two? Simply put, a smoothie is a drink based on fresh, pureed fruit. Juice drinks are only comprised of the liquids extracted from fruits and vegetables (another difference as smoothies contain fruit only). Yet another difference between the two drinks is that smoothies often have a dairy base, such as milk, yoghurt, or ice cream. To make the distinction clear, I have also chosen to include smoothie recipes in this book that have a dairy product as a main ingredient.

I do a juice fast twice a year. For a whole week, I eat and drink nothing except vegetable and fruit juices. I have been doing this for years and I believe that it is very effective for my immune system. There are plenty of recipes in this book that are suitable for juice fasting, all of them delicious drinks made from fresh fruit and vegetables that detoxify your body, leaving you feeling fit and healthy again.

For those with allergies or who don't consume dairy for other reasons, there's no need to despair. You can still enjoy the recipes in this book by replacing the equivalent amount of milk with a non-dairy alternative, such as soy, rice or nut milk. Non-dairy ice cream and yoghurt can also be found in supermarkets and health food stores. The addition of a ripe banana or avocado is also an excellent way to achieve a creamy consistency without using dairy products.

## BASIC SMOOTHIE RECIPE

**For 4 servings**

250 g fruit ✱ 5 dsp yoghurt or milk, buttermilk or ice cream, or a combination of all three of these ingredients.

1. Select one or a combination of soft fruits, such as banana and strawberry.
2. If necessary, peel and stone the fruit then clean and cut the flesh into large pieces.
3. Blend the fruit in a blender or food processor and add the dairy product(s).
4. Blend for 1 to 2 minutes until smooth and frothy, and pour into a glass.

Of course, a juice fast is not always necessary for maintaining good health. Make yourself a tasty juice drink or delicious smoothie each day and that way you get your recommended daily allowance of fruit and vegetables without having to make much effort!

**Children**

Smoothies and juice drinks are also ideal for children. When my children were small they preferred to eat sweets and crisps rather than fruit and vegetables, like most other children. But they were always thirsty when they came home from school or after playing outside. Unbeknownst to them, they still got their intake of the necessary vitamins anyway. This set a good habit for them that has continued into their adult lives because my children still enjoy these healthy drinks.

Since you can put almost anything into juices and smoothies, and this book is also here to inspire you to experiment for yourself, why not encourage your children to join you in making these drinks? Take a look together and see what is in the fridge and fruit bowl. Together, you might just end up creating your own family-favourite recipe.

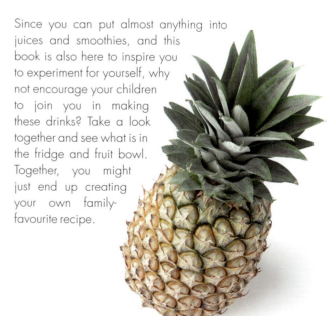

## BASIC RECIPE FOR JUICE DRINKS

Fresh fruit and/or vegetables

1. Peel, stone and clean the fruit and vegetables.
2. Place the ingredients in a juicer (citrus fruits can also be squeezed in a citrus press).
3. Blend the ingredients well.

### Refreshing

I can still remember the fruit tree-filled garden of my youth. For weeks on end, my mother often did nothing other than preserving cherries, berries and many other varieties of fruit. No matter how many jars of jam and preserved fruit disappeared into the fridge and cellar, there was always fruit left over. There was often even too much to eat, and it was definitely a shame to throw away! So have a good look around your garden to see what is growing and blossoming, perhaps you too can then make a delicious, refreshing drink.

No matter how easy it is to make juice drinks and smoothies, it can always be made easier. These days, the shelves in the supermarkets are full of all kinds of healthy drinks. Still, in my opinion, nothing beats the taste of freshly squeezed juice. Aside from the improved flavour, it's also up to you to select the ingredients and their proportions After all, nobody can better decide what is tasty than you!

Drinking fresh juice every day is the ideal way to become healthy and to stay that way. Have a nutritious smoothie for breakfast or a fruit juice drink as a refreshing thirst-quencher. They are the perfect 'pick-me-up' because they are both healthy and extremely delicious.

The best way to drink juice drinks and smoothies is cold, especially in the summertime. So store the fruit in the fridge before you plan to use it (note: bananas change colour very quickly in the fridge).

Ice is also a handy way to chill your drink. Freeze some fruit juice in an ice-cube tray and you will have deliciously refreshing ice cubes. Or add crushed ice to your drink. This not only makes the drink look attractive but it also makes the juice drink nice and cold.

# RECIPES

## JUICE DRINKS

| | |
|---|---|
| Melon-Orange Juice | 14 |
| Nice 'n Fresh | 16 |
| Temptation | 18 |
| Vital Vitamins | 20 |
| Citrus Juice | 22 |
| Cranberry-Apple | 24 |
| Strawberry Passion | 26 |
| Melon breeze | 28 |
| Ruby Red | 30 |
| Cherry Delight | 32 |
| Italian Dream | 34 |
| A Small Experiment | 36 |
| Gazpacho in a Glass | 38 |
| Juicy Salad | 40 |
| Berry Boost | 42 |
| Cucumber-Melon | 44 |
| Mystic mango | 46 |
| Blueberry-apple Juice | 48 |
| Detox Juice | 50 |
| Avocado-Lime Juice | 52 |

## SMOOTHIES

| | |
|---|---|
| Pink lady | 54 |
| Peach-Pear | 56 |
| Fig Smoothie | 58 |
| Choco-Split | 60 |
| Exotic | 62 |
| A taste of Summer | 64 |
| Raspberry Smoothie | 66 |
| Clementine | 68 |
| Tropicana | 70 |
| Strawberry Yoghurt | 72 |
| Banana-Coffee | 74 |
| Kiwi-Buttermilk | 76 |
| Forest Stroll | 78 |
| Yellow Fruit | 80 |
| Nice 'n Cosy | 82 |
| Red Passion | 84 |
| Date-Raisin | 86 |
| Breakfast in a Glass | 88 |
| Cranberry Smoothie | 90 |
| Sweet 'n Sour | 92 |

# MELON-ORANGE JUICE

There are many varieties of melons available. I have chosen to use watermelon and galia melon for this drink because I find that these two flavours work very well together. You can, of course, always choose other varieties of melon if you think that these are tastier and happen to have some in the house. Do take into account, though, that a watermelon contains more juice than most of the other melon varieties, so if you choose a different variety of melon, the chances are that the drink will be thicker.

500 g watermelon * 200 g galia melon * 200 g pineapple * 2 oranges * 1 lime

Put all the ingredients through the juicer and serve chilled

Watermelons are full of minerals and, of course, water. It is one of the easiest foods to digest. To make the most of the health benefits of the watermelon, it is best not to discard the seeds but to use them in the juice drink as they contain extra zinc and vitamin E. A little extra healthiness is always a good thing!

# NICE 'N FRESH

Whenever I make white cabbage salad, I always add some pineapple and ginger. This salad is always a big hit with my friends. The taste is so deliciously fresh that I got to wondering whether it would also be as popular as a recipe for a juice drink. And, as it turns out, the juice drink is just as tasty as the salad.

### half a pineapple ✴ 200 g white cabbage ✴ 2 cm ginger ✴ mint

Put all the ingredients through the * juicer and serve chilled

Ginger has been used for centuries as a natural remedy for improving blood circulation and digestion. It is also effective in relieving colds, infections, nausea, and sore throat. In addition, the mint has a soothing effect, aids the digestion, and helps ease nausea and cramp. What's more, it also helps to relieve bronchial complaints.

# TEMPTATION

The pomegranate is one of the loveliest fruits I know. The seeds are particularly sweet, refreshing and crunchy, and together with the healthy ginger, they make a very unique combination.

2 pears ✱ 4 pomegranates ✱ 2 lemons ✱ 1cm fresh ginger

Put all the ingredients through the juicer and serve chilled

Pomegranates are recognised as a symbol of fertility owing to the abundance of seeds found in the flesh of the fruit. In addition, the pomegranate is inextricably linked with temptation. It has even been claimed that the Tree of Life in the Garden of Eden was, in fact, a pomegranate tree. Eating a pomegranate would therefore have been the reason why Adam and Eve were banished from Paradise.

# VITAL VITAMINS

This is a great juice drink for children. Lots of children dislike vegetables (or at least they say so). But almost all children enjoy apple juice. This drink tastes so refreshing that while you can taste the apples, you cannot taste the carrots that are also included in the recipe. The taste of this drink goes down extremely well with children. Not only is it tasty, but they still get their vital vitamins as well.

250 g carrots * 2 apples * a handful of parsley

Put all the ingredients through the juicer and serve chilled

Parsley has a purifying effect. It is also good for the digestion and the herb provides the entire body with vitamins and minerals.

# CITRUS JUICE

This is a wonderfully tart winter's drink. The honey included in the list of ingredients is really only for people who are not fond of sharp flavours. Taste it for yourself and see which recipe you prefer.

2 oranges * 1 lime * 1 lemon * 2 red grapefruits * mint *
1 tbsp of honey (optional – stir this through the juice if it is too tart for your liking)

Put all the ingredients through the juicer and serve chilled

Lemons are initially used for maintaining a healthy liver and kidneys. In particular, they have an antibacterial and cleansing effect. Lemon juice is also an ideal remedy for heartburn. The lime belongs to the citrus family and has the same health benefits.

# CRANBERRY-APPLE

The island of Terschelling in the Netherlands is known for its many cranberry-based delicacies. During the weekends that I spent there, I tasted as many of these recipes as possible. On one such occasion, I tried a cranberry-apple juice. It was delicious! And once I returned home, I set out in search of the right ingredients and working out the correct proportions. I don't know whether I used exactly the same ingredients as were used in that café, but in any case, the taste is pretty much the same.

2 stalks of celery ✱ 2 apples ✱ 100 g cranberries ✱ ginger ✱ mint

Put all the ingredients through the juicer and add 2 ice cubes. Garnish with a few cranberries.

The story goes that around 1840, beachcomber Pieter-Sipkes Cupido found a barrel on Terschelling beach. He hoped that the barrel was full of strong liquor; however, it turned out to be filled with berries. Disappointed, he emptied the barrel out onto the soil and left the berries behind. The birds spread the seeds of these berries across the island and within a short time, Terschelling was covered in cranberry plants.

# STRAWBERRY PASSION

The name of this drink says it all. If there are strawberries in it, it is always a winner with me, especially if they are Dutch strawberries. Do take into account, though, that strawberries can bring on an allergic reaction in babies and very young children. It is therefore wise to start with very small pieces of strawberry. This way, the body can adapt to them gradually.

500 g strawberries ✻ 2 oranges ✻ 1 lime

Put all the ingredients through the juicer and serve chilled.

Strawberries are one of the most popular and most widely available fruits. They are full of vitamin C and all kinds of minerals, such as calcium. Strawberries are therefore very good for your bones and teeth.

# MELON BREEZE

You might not think so, but mint is delicious when combined with fruit. In this juice drink, it provides a peppery and refreshing taste. Experiment with the quantity of mint you use in the drink. Taste is, and always will be, personal.

1 honey melon ✻ 4 kiwis ✻ 2 lime ✻ small handful of mint

Put all the ingredients through the juicer and serve chilled.

As unattractive as a kiwi is on the outside, it is beautiful on the inside. Kiwis are rich in numerous minerals, such as calcium. What is more, they are full of vitamin C, even more so than most other fruits. Purchase kiwis that are not quite ripe. They will ripen further at home. Do not leave them too long to ripen otherwise they will become much too sweet.

# RUBY RED

Every time I prepare a dish with beetroot, I am enthused by the beautiful red colour of the juice that comes out of it. The colour alone already suggests that it will taste good. I gained my inspiration for this juice drink recipe from a dish with celery and beetroot. The addition of apples and carrots give it an extra refreshing flavour.

**2 red beetroots, raw ∗ 1 cm ginger ∗ 2 stalks of celery ∗ 2 apples ∗ 200 g carrots**

Put all the ingredients through the juicer and serve chilled.

Beetroot juice contains an exceptional amount of vitamins and minerals. According to herbalists, the juice increases the iron content of the blood. When possible, juice the leaves as well because these contain the most vitamins. Beetroot juice boosts the immune system and has been prescribed as a remedy for recovering patients since way back when.

# CHERRY DELIGHT

I can still remember the enormous quantities of cherries that grew in our garden, baskets and baskets full. My mother was forever busy with the preserving jars. I do not preserve fruit myself, but I am quite pleased with my own solution for using up the surplus cherries. They are simply so tasty that it would be a shame to throw them away.

### 600 g cherries ✲ 2 apples ✲ half a cucumber

Put all the ingredients through the juicer and serve chilled.

Did you know that 20 cherries have the same painkilling effect as one aspirin? Some people even believe that cherries can relieve rheumatic pain. The healing power of this fruit has been known for centuries. In days gone by, cherries were also eaten to prevent.

# ITALIAN DREAM

This Italian Dream is extremely suitable as a fasting juice. It is an out-and-out health drink. The basil gives it a peppery flavour and sweet aroma. Experiment yourself to see what proportion suits your taste buds the best. Basil also has a calming effect and is known as a sleep-inducing herb. Drink, enjoy, and relax!

500 g tomatoes ✷ 2 oranges ✷ 2 tbsp dried tomato ✷ a small handful of basil

Put all the ingredients through the juicer and serve chilled.

The tomato is officially classified as a fruit but is considered a vegetable due to its savoury taste. Like basil, tomatoes have a calming effect on the body. What is more, eating tomatoes can reduce liver, prostrate, skin, and digestive complaints.

# A SMALL EXPERIMENT

It normally would not occur to you to put red cabbage through a juicer and certainly not in combination with celery. The inspiration for this drink came to me when I was cooking red cabbage and I noticed just how much juice came out of this vegetable. I thought it would be interesting to experiment with this. The refreshing juice of the celery complements the red cabbage really well, particularly in combination with the juice of the apples and lemon. This is truly a drink to be savoured

> 200 g red cabbage (about half a cabbage) * 2 stalks of celery * 2 apples * 1 lemon
>
> Put all the ingredients through the juicer and serve chilled.

The slightly salty flavour of the celery juice blends very easily with some sweeter flavours, and that is probably the magic of this drink. What is more, celery is also very healthy. It has purifying, calming, and diuretic qualities. The lemon juice completes the taste of this health drink. The lemon juice is heaped with minerals, potassium and vitamin C, and is therefore good for your entire immune system.

# GAZPACHO IN A GLASS

When holidaying in Spain, I always love to sit on a terrace and enjoy the surroundings, the wonderful weather, and a delicious gazpacho. Gazpacho is in fact a drink in itself, however I thought it would be nice to adapt the traditional recipe and create 'gazpacho in a glass' for this book.

> half a red pepper, seeds removed * 500 g tomatoes * half a cucumber * 1 sweet red pepper * 1 tbsp of red wine vinegar * some tomato juice, if necessary
>
> Put all the ingredients through the juicer and serve chilled.

If the juice is too thick, you can add some extra tomato juice or mineral water. The red wine vinegar in this recipe gives the juice a somewhat more intense flavour. The sweet pepper gives it the sweet flavour. Sweet peppers are also an excellent source of antioxidants, vitamin C, and, in particular, beta-carotene.

# JUICY SALAD

The poison green colour alone makes this what I consider to be a very special drink. You probably cannot imagine it, but a lot of juice comes out when you squeeze lettuce. And by adding the other ingredients, it is as if you are eating a complete salad, but then in a glass.

**half a head of iceberg lettuce ✱ 100 g spinach ✱ 1 cucumber, cut half into 'stirring sticks' ✱ 2 apples**

Put all the ingredients through the juicer and serve chilled. Garnish with a 'stirring stick'.

As bland as cucumber can sometimes taste in a salad, the flavour is quite intense when you make a juice from it. To get the optimum benefit it is best to use entire cucumber, skin and all. Most of the vitamins and minerals, such as calcium, zinc, and vitamin K, are found under the skin. This juice drink is particularly suitable as a nightcap. Lettuce is particularly known for its calming qualities. This is an extremely healthy way to get a good nights sleep.

# BERRY BOOST

This is another juice drink that can be enjoyed at any time; on the terrace when the weather is good, with breakfast or in the evening after dinner. Really, you can drink most juices at any time of the day.

### 200 g raspberries ✴ 250 g blueberries ✴ 250 g strawberries

Put all the ingredients through the juicer and serve chilled.

Raspberries contain more healthy substances than most other fruits. Among other things, it seems that raspberries contain a healing substance, which up until now has not been found in such quantities in any other foodstuff. What is more, the flesh is full of vitamin C and other protective antioxidants.

# CUCUMBER-MELON

Sometime you feel like having a juice drink, but don't feel like going to too much effort. This juice drink is ideal for this situation because it requires hardly any preparation in it. Put everything through the juicer and you have a delicious, refreshing drink in no time.

1 cucumber ✱ half a watermelon ✱ a handful of parsley

Put all the ingredients through the juicer and serve chilled.

Although they are made up of 96% water, cucumbers are full of nutrients, such as vitamin A and C, calcium, potassium and sulphur. These minerals help maintain healthy blood pressure, hair and nails. Given that they are virtually calorie-free, cucumbers are especially suitable for people who are dieting.

# MYSTIC MANGO

I find that the delicious flesh of the pineapple is the perfect ingredient for an exotic juice drink. As too are mangos, by the way. As far as I am concerned, no fruit bowl should be without them. Together they form the ultimate combination for me.

half a melon ✳ 1 mango ✳ half a pineapple ✳ 1 lime

Put all the ingredients through the juicer and serve with ice.

Pineapple is full of vitamins and minerals and the flesh contains the substance bromelain. This substance has been found to reduce inflammation in joint disorders.

# BLUEBERRY-APPLE JUICE

As a young girl, I was always secretly nibbling on the blueberries in our garden. I almost always gave myself away however, because the blue juice spilled on to my clothes.

400 g of blueberries * 2 apples

Put the ingredients through the juicer and serve with ice.

The taste of apples varies from sweet to tart, depending on the sort of apples you use. The great thing about apples is that they are available the whole year round and therefore extremely suitable as a basis for juice drinks. Of course, you can also opt to buy ready-made juice from the supermarket, but that won't taste as good freshly squeezed juice. You can add a dash of lemon juice to prevent the freshly as squeezed apple juice from turning brown.

# DETOX JUICE

This is an ideal drink to take during a juice fast. Plums are particularly known for their laxative effect, which gives the body a really good detox. The best time to make this juice drink is early in the autumn when the plums are at their sweetest. This delicious drink is easy to make and has an irresistible aroma.

600 g of plums ✱ 400 g blue grapes, preferably seedless ✱ 2 limes ✱ 2 tbsp of honey ✱ 1 tbsp of thyme

Put all the ingredients through the juicer and serve with ice.

Grapes are fairly watery and are therefore a good supplement to almost any vegetable or fruit drink. Traditionally, grape juice is a homeopathic calming remedy. What is more, it seems that grape juice relieves the symptoms of arthritis and helps to detox the body, which makes the juice extra suitable as a fasting juice.

# AVOCADO-LIME JUICE

Yet another juice drink where you do not know what the end result will taste like. It is often a question of trial and error until you find the tastiest combination. I experimented with various ingredients for this juice. I felt that there was something missing until I added the basil. Then the drink was complete.

3 ripe avocados * 1 cucumber * basil * 2 limes

Put all the ingredients through the juicer and serve with ice.

Well-ripened avocados give a creamy consistency to the juice. They are often used to replace dairy products. This is particularly ideal for people with lactose intolerance, and very healthy as well. Avocados are full of vitamin E, an essential vitamin for healthy skin.

# PINK LADY

While I find that rhubarb is lovely, it is, at the same time, a dangerous vegetable. The leaf of the rhubarb is highly poisonous and you should therefore never use it. The rest of the vegetable is very tasty. Make sure that you cook the rhubarb first. You cannot process this vegetable for a drink or smoothie if it is raw.

> 200 g rhubarb, cut into chunks and cooked ✻ 1 tbsp of sugar ✻ 300 g strawberries ✻ 1 tbsp of honey ✻ the juice of 2 oranges ✻ 5 dsp cold milk

1. Mix the rhubarb chunks with the sugar and leave the mixture to stand for about 1 hour.
2. Stir the strawberries into the mixture and bring to the boil. Leave to cool and then place it in the fridge for a few hours.
3. Puree the fruit, honey, and orange juice in the blender.
4. Add the cold milk and puree until frothy.

Rhubarb has a naturally tart taste. If, in spite of the added sugar, you feel that this smoothie tastes too sharp, you can always add some extra sugar or honey.

# PEACH-PEAR

This is a particularly good drink if you want to give your body a good detox. The apples as well as the pears have a powerful detoxification effect. Many people associate healthy smoothies with an unpleasant taste. This peach-pear recipe proves otherwise.

2 peaches * 2 apples * 2 pears * 2½ dsp milk * 2½ dsp yoghurt

Blend all the ingredients in the blender.

The high beta-carotene content in peaches helps protect the lungs and improve skin and digestive complaints. They are also very good for the eyes. Peaches are easily digested, but they also have a slightly laxative and diuretic effect, so do not eat too many of them.

# FIG SMOOTHIE

It was a really enjoyable challenge for me to make a smoothie with figs. They are not particularly juicy, so it is better to combine them with other juices, in this case, orange, grapefruit and lime juice.

6 large ripe figs * the juice of 2 oranges * the juice of 2 red grapefruits * 2 dsp milk * 1 tbsp of honey * the juice of 1 lime * crushed ice

1. Cut off the hard bits of the stalk of the figs and slice in two.
2. Pour the orange juice, grapefruit juice, and milk into a blender and add the figs and honey. Blend the ingredients to a smooth consistency.
3. Add the lime juice and blend briefly. Serve with crushed ice.

Figs are extremely healthy, particularly if you suffer from bronchial irritation. Do, however, take into account that figs have a strong laxative effect, so do not eat too many of them.

# CHOCO-SPLIT

When my children were young, it was always a real treat for them when they were given a banana split. This is still a tasty dessert, for young and old. Chocolate is an irresistible ingredient and it tastes absolutely fantastic combined with banana and ice cream. I was very curious to see how this combination would work in a smoothie. And it turns out that it is even tastier than the dessert.

**1 dspl chocolate sauce ✻ 2 bananas ✻ 1 tbsp of cocoa powder ✻ 2½ dsp vanilla ice cream ✻ 2½ dsp milk**

Blend all the ingredients in the blender.

While you cannot juice bananas, they do make a wonderful basis for smoothies. The banana makes the smoothie a meal in itself. What is more, bananas are full of soft fibres that are good for the intestines and they provide lots of energy.

# EXOTIC

What is nice and surprising about this smoothie is that it has a little bit of bite to it due to the addition of the passionfruit seeds. This gives it a crunchy texture, which you would not expect of a drink. Initially, I left out the seeds, but I was really curious how it would taste if I added them. The result was delicious!

1 papaya ✱ 2 pieces of Sharon fruit ✱ 3 passionfruits, seeds removed (do not discard the seeds) ✱ the juice of 2 oranges ✱ 4 dsp yoghurt

Blend all the ingredients in the blender and stir in the passion fruit seeds at the last moment.

The papaya is known as a tropical wonder fruit, full of vitamin C, fibres, and enzymes that aid the digestive system. Passionfruit is also a good source of vitamin C. The more ugly and wrinkled the fruit is, the more fuller and juicer it tastes. The passionfruit has a strong aroma, which is clearly noticeable in this smoothie.

# A TASTE OF SUMMER

Whenever I drink this, I can taste the summer. During the day in the sun or on a muggy summer evening, this is the ideal refreshment for me. I think this is because of the sparkle of orange going through it.

> 500 g mixed summer fruits, set aside 4 tbsp for garnishing ✽ 3 dsp freshly squeezed orange juice ✽ 2 dsp milk

> Blend all the ingredients in the blender and garnish with summer fruits that were set aside earlier.

Orange juice is a classic fruit juice, a common sight on supermarket shelves. But still, nothing beats the taste of freshly squeezed juice, full of vitamin C. Orange juice is often used as a remedy for colds and flu. It is also full of folic acid and that is good for the heart and blood cells.

# RASPBERRY SMOOTHIE

This smoothie is sweet and refreshing, exactly how raspberries are supposed to taste. When using raspberries, do take into account that it is a particularly fragile fruit. Rinse them carefully and, if necessary, pat dry, this way they will still look enticing if you want to use some for garnishing.

200 g raspberries ✱ 2 apples ✱ 2 pears ✱ 5 dsp buttermilk

Blend all the ingredients in the blender.

Raspberries are a particularly rich source of nutrients, especially antioxidants. Raspberry juice purifies the digestive tract. Traditionally, the juice is used for treating diarrhoea, indigestion, and rheumatism.

# CLEMENTINE

This is a real vitamin bomb – delicious, very simple and extremely healthy. When they were young, I used to always give this to my children if they had a touch of the flu. It is also a good solution for using up the large quantity of clementines that come in a net sack. Peel the lot in one go and use to make a delicious smoothie.

### 6 clementines * 5 dsp buttermilk * small amount of honey (optional)

### Blend all the ingredients in the blender.

This smoothie tastes just as good without the honey, and it is then also a little healthier.

Clementines are a cross between several citrus fruits. They have an aromatic, sweet taste and are less tart than oranges. They have the same health qualities as oranges and their juice is ideal to use as a basis for any drink.

# TROPICANA

The first time that I drank this smoothie was while on holiday in Aruba. I was immediately sold. Use fresh fruit as this will do justice to the flavours of the pineapple and melon. When I drink this, I feel like I am on holiday again. And that is a feeling that you just cannot beat!

half a pineapple ✱ half a melon ✱ 2½ dsp vanilla ice cream ✱ 2½ dsp yoghurt

Blend all the ingredients in the blender.

Fresh pineapple is a good remedy for digestive complaints and cleanses the digestive tract by killing off the dead cells. The enzymes in pineapple also help to purify your blood. The flesh of the pineapple can help to reduce back pain, relieve arthritic pain, and dissolve excess mucus.

Pineapples are ripe when they are slightly soft to the touch, smell good and the green spots have disappeared. The leaves should be firm and green and the tips should not be yellow.

# STRAWBERRY YOGHURT

I find that the combination of strawberries and yoghurt always tastes good. Whether it is summer, winter, autumn or spring, you should always take care to purchase quality fruit. Always try to buy brightly coloured, plump strawberries and wash them just before you use them. This brings out the wonderful flavour of this special fruit at its best.

500 g fresh strawberries * the juice of 1 grapefruit * 1 banana * 1 tbsp of honey * 5 dsp yoghurt

Blend all the ingredients in the blender.

Strawberries usually taste sweet with a slightly sharp undertone. They are at their best and sweetest when they are ripe. Strawberries contain substances that give your body a good detox and thorough cleansing.

# BANANA-COFFEE

My ideal way to wake up is with a nice cup of coffee. I set the busyness of the day aside for a while and begin the day quietly. If I have the time and really want to spoil myself then I make this smoothie. My delicious cup of coffee combined with fruit and ice. I would be quite happy to start every day like this.

2 dsp milk ✳ 4 tbsp of instant coffee ✳ 3 dsp vanilla ice cream ✳ 2 bananas

1. Pour the milk into the blender and add the instant coffee. Blend thoroughly.
2. Add the ice cream and bananas and puree the mixture until it is a smooth and frothy drink.

As is the case with most fruit, the riper the banana is, the fuller the taste. Bananas are excellent for using in smoothies even when they are overripe. They are ideal for giving drinks a thicker and fuller consistency. This makes them ideal for people who are intolerant to dairy products. Even if a smoothie contains no dairy produce, it will still have a creamy consistency.

# KIWI-BUTTERMILK

I absolutely love tart-tasting foods and therefore buttermilk is one of my favourite dairy drinks. The combination with the sharp flavour of the kiwis makes this the ultimate smoothie for me. An acquired taste for some perhaps, but it is delicious.

**4 kiwis ∗ the juice of 1 orange ∗ 5 dsp buttermilk**

Blend all the ingredients in the blender.

Buttermilk is virtually fat free and contains as much calcium as ordinary milk. Ideal for people who are dieting or who want to pay more attention to their health. Replace the milk in any recipe with buttermilk and you cannot go far wrong.

# FOREST STROLL

Around August, we used to always go into the woods with the whole family to pick bilberries. We brought along buckets to carry the fruit and filled them all to the brim. There were more than enough berries to go around, so just as many berries went into our mouths. We went home with full stomachs as well as full buckets!

250 g bilberries * 250 g blackberries * 2 dsp yoghurt * 1 dsp vanilla ice cream

Blend all the ingredients in the blender.

It is always said of bilberries that they are good for the eyes. Pilots during the Second World War ate lots of bilberries because they believed that this improved their night vision. Bilberries do, in any case, certainly contain lots of antioxidants, which boost the immune system.

Unfortunately, the amount of wild bilberries has decreased in recent years. You can still find blackberries, though. Blackberries contain a lot of vitamin C and therefore, like the bilberry, boost the immune system. Blackberries are also an important source of calcium and are good for the nervous system.

# YELLOW FRUIT

This is an ideal smoothie to accompany you while sitting outside and daydreaming on the balcony. Close your eyes, take a sip and let the multitude of flavours transport you to the tropics.

300 g of pineapple ✶ 200 g mango ✶ 1 banana ✶ the juice of 2 limes ✶ 2 dsp yoghurt ✶ 2 dsp coconut milk ✶ 1 dsp milk

Blend all the ingredients in the blender.

The best time to buy mangos is when they are ripe and are slightly soft when you press them. To avoid disappointment, select your mangos carefully: if they are not ripe or are too ripe, the taste will just not be the same and that would be a shame. Mangos have an aromatic, rich flavour and combined with the banana and pineapple make a delicious, tropical smoothie.

# BILBERRY

This smoothie reminds me of winter. It really is a drink to cosy up with when it is too cold to go outside. Not only is it delicious but it provides you with the necessary vitamins to help see you through the cold winter months.

400 g bilberries ✱ 4 apples ✱ the juice of 1 lime ✱ 1 tbsp of honey ✱ 5 dsp yoghurt

Blend all the ingredients in the blender.

Crisp, tart apples are the most suitable for making smoothies. They are a perfect basis for fruit juice and are extremely healthy due to the many vitamins, minerals, fibres, and malic acid they contain. Apples are not only good for detoxification, they also lower the cholesterol, are good for the skin and aid the digestion. Some varieties of apple are rich in vitamin C and therefore help to boost the immune system and to prevent flu.

# RED PASSION

What excites me about this drink is the addition of coconut milk. Everyone is familiar with the flavour of the red fruits; however, generally speaking, not everyone is familiar with the flavour of coconut. This drink is a tasty way to introduce the wonderful flavour of coconut.

100 g raspberries * 100 g strawberries * 200 g red currants * 2 dsp coconut milk * 2 dsp yoghurt * 1 dsp vanilla ice cream

Blend all the ingredients in the blender.

Many people think that coconut milk is the watery liquid that is found in the coconut. This is not the case. Coconut milk is a liquid that is obtained by mixing grated coconut with warm water and then straining it. The watery liquid found in the coconut is simply coconut water.

# DATE-RAISIN

This smoothie is ideal if you have hardly any fresh fruit in the house. Since dried fruit cannot be processed into a juice on it's own, you must first soak the dates, prunes, and raisins. If you soak this fruit first in hot water or, for example, tea, you will have a sweet juice that you can then use to make the most delicious smoothies.

30 g dried dates, soaked * 70 g prunes, soaked * 50 g raisins, soaked * the juice of 2 grapefruits * 3 dsp milk * 2 dsp yoghurt

Blend all the ingredients in the blender.

The sharper the grapefruits that are used in this smoothie, the more refreshing it will taste. Do not peel or remove the pith from the grapefruit but include it in the drink. These are full of vitamin C and all sorts of other antioxidants that are good for your immune system. It would be a shame to let these go to waste.

# BREAKFAST

It is a bit boring to eat ordinary muesli with yoghurt every day. This smoothie is a nice alternative, particularly if you want to have breakfast in bed but hate all the crumbs that are usually left behind!

> 1cm fresh ginger ✱ 2 tbsp ginger syrup ✱ 50 g pre-soaked dried apricots ✱ 80 g muesli, set aside 2 tablespoons for garnishing ✱ 3 dsp low-fat milk
>
> Blend all the ingredients in the blender.

You can buy muesli from the supermarket, but you can also make it yourself: roast some grain flakes, nuts, and seeds for 15 minutes at 150°C/gas mark 2/300 Fahrenheit. After roasting, you can add some fresh or dried fruit for flavour.

# CRANBERRY-SMOOTHIE

Cranberries are often used to prevent or cure cystitis or other urinary infections. For this purpose, you should drink a little juice for a couple of days consecutively. The antioxidants in the berries specifically target the bacteria in the urinary passages and prevent them from causing damage.

> 400 g young rhubarb, cut into 2cm pieces, cooked and cooled down * 1 banana * 1 apple * 100 g sugar * 100 g fresh cranberries * 4 dsp milk
>
> Blend all the ingredients in the blender.

The healing power of the cranberry has been known to the Native North Americans for centuries. They used the juice to protect against bladder infection, to treat arrow wounds and it for dyeing their clothes.

# SWEET 'N SOUR

What I really like about this smoothie is the combination of sweet and tart flavours. As a real fan of sharp flavours, I don't bother adding the honey. If your taste buds tend to the sweet, then by all means include it. That's the great thing about smoothies, you can experiment for yourself and use your imagination to create your own personal favourite.

400 g watermelon ✱ 200 g galia melon ✱ 1 tbsp honey ✱ 5 dsp buttermilk

Blend all the ingredients in the blender.

There are several ways to check if a melon is ripe. A ripe melon should smell sweet and fragrant. A watermelon is ripe if it sounds hollow when you tap the fruit. Melons cleanse the digestive tract, are good for skin complaints, and have a diuretic effect. The seeds are rich in potassium, which helps to reduce high blood pressure. It is therefore best not to discard these seeds, but to use them in your smoothie.